TABLE OF CONTENTS

INTRODUCTION

UNDERSTANDING THE WORD

Throughout life, we come across all sorts of people. We might find ourselves in the presence of people who bring us great things, such as positive vibes and enriching experiences, but we may likewise find ourselves in the presence of people who aren't wishing the best for us or some who don't have our best interest at heart. We may equally find ourselves surrounded by people who are, in fact, focused on impacting our lives in a way that isn't conducive to positive outcomes but rather the opposite. As such, we face these rivals, these 'enemies,' so to speak, and we must know how to limit the influence they may be having over our lives.

Now, what makes a person a rival? What is a "rival," after all? Is it necessarily a person, or is it perhaps a challenge that is set in your way? How would you conceptualize a rival? This is what we will be discussing throughout this book, namely while trying to explore the various conceptualizations of the term. The people you meet in your day-to-day life are likely to bring you all sorts of challenges, and whether or not these contribute to your self-development and your growth as a human being is what we will be exploring

These rivals may influence your life in both good and bad ways, or in only one of those. For example, you may end up with a rival who is there to push you to surpass your own capacity, something they may do by pushing you to question what you find important or not. You may face this kind of rivalry when you need to be challenged or when you have gotten too deep into your comfort zone. Maybe you are getting so used to being where you are that this rival comes in and makes you feel like you are missing out on life's many opportunities - some that could be achieved if you only took the time to push yourself to try and surpass this rival. As such, a bit of healthy competition is never a bad thing. On the other hand, giving up because you feel like this rival is getting everything that you've ever wanted, or giving up because you feel like it isn't worth the hassle, isn't the right way to welcome a rival into your life.

Aside from this, what could a rival mean? Perhaps it means understanding that certain people are cancerous in your life, or almost like a parasite. They may hang onto you and try to drag you down with them, even if they know that they aren't good for you at all. For example, this happens a lot when we are younger: we surround ourselves with the wrong crowd in an attempt to fit in. Perhaps we feel lost, so we end up assimilating with those who make us feel at home, even if we only end up with them because they are toxic and are "recruiting," so to speak, others to include in their circle. This is often the case when we surround ourselves with people who don't want what's best for us, but instead, people who want to see us make the same wrong choices as they are making so as not to feel so alone in their misery. We often see this in toxic relationships, friend circles that support each other's bad decisions, and so on. We see this time and time again, and unfortunately, many get swept up in this negative cycle. So, rivals don't always need to be people who you are jealous of or people you are in competition with fact; they may be the people you shouldn't be in competition with or those who show you an example of the kind of lifestyle choice you should be avoided at all costs.

Even then, your definition of a "rival" may differ from that of others. Whereas I see a rival as a person, event, or situation, you may see it as merely a person who is standing in your way or someone who represents competition. Perhaps rivalry, to you, holds a mainly negative connotation that makes you feel like you want to avoid it at all costs; whereas to others, having a rival is symbolic of something much more positive, namely being lucky enough to have someone in life who stands there and pushes one to go further.

As such, before you move any further in this book, perhaps it is a good idea to ask yourself, what is a rival to you? What do you think of when you think about a rival? What do you consider a positive challenge and a negative one? When you have these rivals, they either get you to go forward and push yourselves to new fronts simply because your inner competitiveness wants to see you succeed and emerge as the winner, or they get you to crumble down. The main difference between the two? Whether you have a mindset focused on growth or one focused on stability - a fixed mindset.

What you see as being a "rival" will affect your understanding of the next few chapters. So, take a moment now to try to conceptualize it. Think of various examples: experiences that made you feel like you were pushing against the situation and trying to emerge as a winner, people who made you feel like you were less than, and times in life where you know you perhaps gave up too easily, or where you may not have held on long enough because you didn't feel like you were up to par. This book will challenge these assumptions. We'll start by understanding where this innate feeling stems from, how it can fuel you and how it can break you, and how the success you experience is completely dependent on the moves you make and the timing you opt for. Aside from this, we will be looking at how the people who surround you make you who you are and how they can either encourage you or pull you down - in other words, your vibe attracts your tribe, and vice versa. We'll then discuss finding out who you are, namely through the art of growing your self-awareness and then how you can become a better you with the right vision and the emotional intelligence to remain grounded. Finally, we'll discuss your family, finding those who you trust and want to have around, and how it shares the world you want to live in as well as your legacy.

CHAPTER ONE

YOU'RE BORN WITH IT!

When we speak about having rivals in life, we have different expectations of what facing a "rival" may entail. For example, a rival to you, maybe Thomas from the 8th grade, as he bullied you and made you feel like you were very small. Perhaps he made fun of you while you were on the basketball court as you were a bit shorter than the others. And then, when you were back home at night, you'd imagine yourself a few inches taller and winning the games with your 3-pointer shot, or better yet, dribbling between his legs. Take that, Thomas! Okay, back to real life - your rival is not only a rival because it is someone who seems to be doing better than you. In this case, it is someone whose actions are threatening your livelihood. In fact, there is an interesting biological and sociological explanation behind this rivalry.

See, hundreds, if not thousands of years ago, we were mainly separated into social groups considered "tribes." These tribes are just like the kinds of tribes you are thinking of, such as the Masaai in various parts of Sub-Saharan Africa, which are indeed a good way of comparing things. Back in the day when urbanization had not taken place fully, and when we still relied on our communities greatly to survive, rivalry existed but was indeed a different concept. Whereas individual rivalry is currently quite common, especially because of the way we live as societies, back when we lived as tribes or even just in villages, there was no space for it. Instead, a rivalry was found between various communities where one would perhaps fight another for the resources it had access to, among other reasons.

This brings me to the crux of this chapter: although rivalry was present between communities, it was also somewhat present within these, but not as you may think. The rivalry was not based on figuring out who had the most power or who was the best within the community. Instead, there was a need to fit the requirements set out by the community to be allowed to remain in it. In other words, ensuring that one would remain in the community was the main point of focus, as this community meant survival. Without the strength and support that was brought by numbers, one was much more likely to die, mainly because the community served as both a safety net and a solid group that would commonly act in solidarity. As such, without this tight-knit community, one was left alone to fend for oneself, something that was much more likely to lead to failure if another community or tribe (or wild animal) came for them. Although perhaps an abstract concept, it does explain well why the rivalry is something we see when we fear for our social

Position. When we are bullied or when we feel like others aren't accepting us within their social group, we may see them as a rival because they are actively putting our survival in danger. This innate feeling is one that has grown with us, and although we may not need a community to help us survive wild animal attacks anymore, we still have a need for social belonging and human interaction. As such, interactions that threaten this safety, and situations that make us feel like we may lose the security of having a group of people protecting us, create a feeling of rivalry. You feel like you need to do everything needed to overcome the potential danger that accompanies this.

There are other forms of rivalry, however. For example, as human beings, we are also born with a competitive nature. When we did not have these tribes, or when we indeed had to fend for ourselves in order to survive, we had no choice but to compete for it. This hasn't changed all that much: we compete with others to get the best jobs, which is now our form of survival. Without a job, we can’t thrive. We may be able to survive, but it's difficult to have a life that is enjoyable. Otherwise explained, although we may indeed survive without these basics, as human beings, it is in our nature to avoid friction as much as possible. We attempt to have the best lifestyle possible, especially the most comfortable one while reducing the amount of effort needed to achieve it. We do so to conserve energy for later, namely, to avoid the possibility that we may end up having too little energy to survive. As such, the game of rivalry is not only one that is modern and influenced by the societal expectation we see today, but rather, it is one that is deeply rooted in our human nature that focuses on survival.

We see this in nature, too: animals compete so they can mate with the optimal partner, and/or they fight over the resource they need to access. We, as animals, are competitive in nature. We want what's best for ourselves, and we need to access the right basics to survive. When our survival is threatened, such as when we are at risk of losing our community or access to the resources we need to live, we then deal with rivalry. Finally, a rival maybe someone that triggers our fight-or-flight system inside when we fear that our survival is in danger because our primal instincts kick in. This follows a Maslowian perspective on survival, namely a theory outlining how human beings are motivated to survive and live according to their wishes.

The hierarchy of needs concept is the central organizing principle for the psychology of human beings. In general, according to Maslow, there are five basic levels of needs: physiological needs, safety needs, love, and belonging needs, esteem needs, and self-actualization needs. According to this theory, as people feel that they have adequately satisfied their basic physiological needs, higher ones, such as self-esteem, start to emerge. Self-esteem, in particular, may be referred to as the top level of needs but follows that of belonging, which we discussed above in more depth. People who are higher up in the hierarchy of needs feel that they are capable of being satisfied with their lives and, as such, feel more fulfilled as human beings. When these physiological needs aren't fulfilled, it is usually followed by an attempt to get these in order before anything else - scavenging for food, attempting to build shelter from any possible means, etc. When these are fulfilled, we can start to be more attentive to the other needs, which each entail a part of rivalry: you are a rival to others when trying to remain safe, feel loved and like you belong, build esteem, and self-actualize.

To wrap up the ideas we've covered so far, try and understand how you may be rivaling others in your life simply out of pure human nature. How often do you give your all to someone or a situation because you fear the repercussions of not doing so? How often are you a rival to others because you feel that they may be the key to belonging or being a part of the community? Alternatively, have you found yourself in situations where you questioned yourself and your capacity to succeed because your self-esteem had taken a hit? Situations, just like people, can act as rivals. They can make you feel like you are completely in control but can just as easily take this control away from you, leaving you at a loss. When challenges emerge, it is up to you to either see them as opportunities to learn and grow or as some that are only there to bring negativity. In other words, your mindset and how you perceive this rival - either as something great that you can learn from or something that hinders your potential for success - is a key player in your concrete experience of the world. How you handle this rivalry is hence what we need to focus on, so let's dive in.

CHAPTER TWO

RIVALRY FUELS YOU

Life with challenges is uncomfortable but overcoming those presented will help make your life more fulfilling and meaningful. You will become a happier person and enjoy the journey more instead of constantly worrying about what could have been or what could have failed - you'll have experienced it, and that in itself is gratifying. The growth mindset that comes with overcoming challenges will make you want to go on and do even more to reach your goals.

Rivalry, as we have established, is not necessarily indicative of a contest between you and someone else. It can, in fact, be a contest within yourself. Feeling like a rival to yourself is often one of the biggest reasons why people give up - the idea of overcoming challenges is overwhelming and may simply feel impossible to achieve. As such, it becomes easier to not try at all and hence to avoid failure altogether than to take on the rival and push with as much force as possible. That's typical of a fixed mindset. On the other hand, you have a growth mindset: one that helps fuel you and pushes you to keep going, even when you feel like it's not worth it.

Rivalry can indeed be something instead of someone. You can have a rivalry with yourself, for example, when you feel like you need to overcome a certain challenge and feel as though the only person standing in the way is yourself. You may feel like you are constantly being challenged by life, or as though whatever is going on in life, you have perpetual challenges in your way that simply keep you on your toes at all times of the day. If this is the case, then indeed, you are in rivalry with yourself! The situations you experience and the hardships you face each count as a form of rivalry. You have to compete with yourself. Will you take on the challenge, or will you focus on keeping things as stable and trouble-free as possible? Will you look for ways to better the situation that involves you taking a leap of faith, or will you give in to the situation and accept it as the new normal? This is what is meant when I speak about adopting a growth mindset: taking each challenge and even failure as a potential opportunity for you to learn.

There's a common misnomer that those who possess a growth mindset do not face difficulties but instead are immune to them. This couldn't be further from the truth. Individuals with this mindset struggle throughout their lives, but it is not because they don't have the chance to overcome obstacles; rather, it is due to the mindset that is pushing them forward. Individuals who possess this kind of mindset view setbacks and challenges as a way of life that they must learn to conquer and are people who are not able to stop or turn away from a challenge. They are their own rivals, and they revel in this information.

A growth mindset refers to an approach to thinking that will help you achieve your goals and develop a positive, forward-thinking attitude where you beat your own competition yourself by propelling you forward towards big accomplishments. Individuals with the opposite mindset - the fixed mindset - believe that their capabilities are what they are and that no amount of hard work will change that; therefore, they tend to give into rivalry and don't work to become better versions of themselves. Instead, those with a growth mindset believe that their talents, hard work, and persistence will determine the result and, therefore, that no challenge or rival can ever stop their growth.

One essential trait of the growth mindset is the ability to look at failures as learning experiences. Individuals who adopt this belief can learn from their mistakes and grow from them; therefore, they welcome these rather than being afraid of the potential struggle ahead. Instead of seeing failure as a permanent setback, individuals who cultivate this mindset view it as a chance to better themselves. Similarly, instead of becoming discouraged and withdrawing themselves from such situations, individuals who embrace learning and growth embrace failure and use it as a steppingstone to becoming even more capable and successful than they ever imagined possible. As such, rivalry fuels them instead of bringing them down.

Another trait of a growth mindset believes that you are not alone in facing challenges, but rather that there is an entire world out there making mistakes and experiencing the same challenges that you are facing When individuals cultivate this mindset, they do not view every situation as a challenge, but rather, view each situation as a new opportunity. By embracing a mindset that makes you focus on beating yourself as your own competition by focusing on how your own thoughts could be holding you back, you can look at the positives and maximize from the negatives. Cultivating this mindset gives you the ability to take advantage of all challenges and opportunities that come your way, rather than just accepting your fate, and moving on to the next thing after giving up.

The final trait of the growth mindset is the ability to stop seeking immediate gratification. Individuals who embrace this mindset believe that the quality of the results does not necessarily depend on how hard the effort is but rather the quality of the thoughts and the planning that you do before you begin. Individuals who do not embrace this mindset believe that by trying harder, they can force the outcome to be different, which oftentimes is not true. By embracing a growth mindset, you stop seeking immediate satisfaction and instead choose to enjoy the process and the outcomes that you get along the way, not only the final product.

It's important to understand and accept that you will most likely experience failures in your lifetime, but overcoming these obstacles requires taking complete control of your self-perspective and preparing yourself to deal with the fear of failure rather than hoping for a change without prompt action. Without this, you'll shut yourself off to new and creative opportunities because you'll have your mind on how you may fail instead of doing what you know you can and should do. In other words, while you may be afraid of certain outcomes based on previous experiences or irrational fear of an outcome being less than desirable, you shouldn't let it affect the actions you are taking. You should, instead, focus on being strong and convince yourself that whatever you face, you can handle it.

Through this mindset, you rise. You become a version of yourself that is not influenced by any other rival than yourself. You see each person, hard situation, or difficult moment in your life as a potential way for you to learn and grow as a person. When you meet people who make you feel like you aren't good enough or as though they are better than you, instead of shutting down, you ask yourself, why do I feel this way? Why do I let others make me feel this way? What can I do to change this feeling within me? Why can't I just be me without this negative feeling? And then, you get answers. You start working with these answers, and you learn and grow as a person.

There is another side to this medal, however. Rivalry, just like it can fuel you to become your best self, can also make you fall. It can make you doubt yourself. This happens in two ways: you either doubt yourself by letting your own rivalry pin you against yourself, or you let others break you. When limiting beliefs and negative self-talk settle in, it can be very difficult to deal with rivalry as you let your biggest competition win: yourself. Thus, overcoming these negative ideas brought on by your own thoughts and most likely influenced by how others speak to you - or about you - is key. On the other hand, when facing rivals that only want the worst for you is on the cards, you also need to be ready to take the challenge on.

Some people only want to eliminate the purity in you. It's up to you to make sure you don't let them!

CHAPTER THREE

IT BREAKS YOU

While rivalry can fuel you, as we have seen in the previous chapter, it can similarly hinder you from being able to achieve what you have in mind, and it can break you. Rivalry, when you cannot emerge as the winner, can make you fall on your knees and may take away every ounce of self-esteem you have. Unless you can adopt the growth mindset as discussed previously, you may struggle to see a learning opportunity in the challenge. However, something even more crucial emerges here: can you face your own darkness? Can you stop yourself from taking your own purity away? How many negative thoughts do you entertain about yourself, some that may be holding you back from beating this rival and overcoming challenges? Perhaps you feel like you are a positive-minded person. But think about this: do you find yourself thinking of yourself as less than others? When others are mean or say rude things to you, do you prefer taking yourself out of the situation completely, or do you face the situation? The former may indicate that you're letting rivals break you! Thus, this chapter will focus exactly on this, namely understanding exactly how you may be letting your rivals win. How do others hold power over you? Perhaps by leading you to believe that you are not good enough, not talented enough, and so on? As such, a key aspect of taking back control is limiting the extent to which you allow others' opinions to affect you and demoralize you. This is done by acknowledging two things: your negative self-talk and your limiting beliefs. So, let's explore these concepts in more detail.

Self-talk describes what you think about yourself and your own ability to succeed at something. For example, if someone tells you that you are too slow to learn something, you might criticize yourself for being unable to grasp things quickly after this - you transfer what others have said about you into self-talk, although it does not always have to stem from there. On the other hand, if you tell yourself that you are good enough, then you'll focus on your positive qualities and forget to criticize yourself. These negative beliefs create negative self-talk and vice versa, which affects how you may choose to keep going forward or not. It may seem like a small thing, but that small voice can affect you much more than you may think.

Negative self-talk is something we all experience from time to time. It may sound reasonable ("I'm not very good at this, so I should avoid trying it for my own personal safety"), or it can be outright mean ("I can never do this. It's such a waste of time. I can't do anything right!"). The problem with negative self-talk, whether you experience it regularly or on occasion, is that it becomes embedded into your thought processes and essentially becomes a part of who you are. Here's the deal: Most of us have experiences that bring negative thoughts into our consciousness. Things like feeling helpless, angry, resentful, depressed, guilty, and so on. When these things arise in our lives, they usually trigger our negative thinking patterns. At first, these negative habits may feel pretty harmless and even beneficial - they push us to think, "Hey, that's not, right? don't think this way". Eventually, though, these negative thoughts, or habits, can grow into something called "self-defeating thoughts" or behavior.

You need to consciously alter your beliefs. Cognitive restructuring is one way to do this. Cognitive restructuring involves rewiring your brain with positive affirmations, healthy self-talk, and new ways of thinking. To make this work, you must start with positive self-talk, replacing negative thoughts with positive ones that support yourself instead of allowing the rival to thrive. Affirmations can help change your view of rivalry altogether: pushing you to adopt the growth mindset we discussed earlier.

It's important to realize that using negative self-talk can be healthy sometimes. Sometimes, your negative self-talk can motivate you to pursue your goals and overcome a rival. It may frustrate you so much to have low self-esteem that you use it as a motivator to better yourself and emerge as a winner. However, without this switch in mindset, negative self-talk can keep you stuck in a harmful cycle, causing you to stay stuck and unable to overcome this rivalry. In fact, when negative self-talk starts to hold you back without you even noticing, we call this a "limiting belief."

How many limiting beliefs do you have? Chances are, you don't know. One thing's for sure: They stop you from succeeding in life. It takes work and self-discipline to get rid of your limiting beliefs, but it's possible. And it all starts by understanding what they are. Limiting beliefs are usually thoughts, beliefs, or opinions that hold you back from pursuing your goals. You might think that your job is boring and that you don't have the skills to succeed at work - these limit you from doing your best and gaining the most out of the experience. Or you might think that you are not good enough at sports and that you'll never play football well, so you drop out after the second training. You might even hold the belief that you are just not smart enough to get into a particular college, so you don't bother applying. In other words, limiting beliefs keep you from doing what you want to do, but the worst part? You are your own enemy in this ordeal.

The first thing you need to do is to reframe these limiting beliefs. Rather than thinking that they are true, imagine what would happen if you embraced the opposite. Imagine a world where you are successful at work and enjoy it every day. Or imagine a world where you don't care about your potential failure in football, but you still stick around because, well, why not?! Reframing your limiting beliefs allows your wishes and more positive perspectives of yourself to become your reality instead of something that helps your enemy win. In other words, it is a small change that can bring you to start seeing yourself as a person who is competent and capable of amazing things. When you let yourself stop your own development and your own personal growth, you are making yourself your biggest enemy. What a shame, as this is the one thing you have control over! In a world full of people who will want to see you fail and who may even work hard to see this happen, why would you make yourself your biggest rival?

As such, when you let yourself become a rival that pushes you down, instead of bringing you up as you do with a growth mindset, you are effectively allowing yourself to break down. You are letting yourself fall. Instead, what if you worked on developing yourself, namely your self-worth and confidence, and then executed the right plan of attack? Wouldn't that be more efficient? Ideally, yes! So, let's talk about getting the timing right.

CHAPTER FOUR

IT'S ABOUT THE ACTIONS YOU TAKE

When we think about the kinds of times where you may face rivalry, we may have different perspectives of what they mean. For example, you may look at the experiences you are going through that make you feel like nothing is worth continuing on for, but in reality, these experiences have been put exactly in your way for that reason. They have been placed there, whether by a God if you a religious or by fate if you aren't - to test you and see how far you can go. Now, this all depends on the perspective you have on this matter. Are the experiences you are living through the result of someone putting them there in your way, or are they simply a game of luck? Otherwise, do they result from the choices you have made? In any case, the experience you will have afterward will completely depend on the moves you make.

So, what do we mean by "the moves you make"? What could this possibly mean? The moves you make in the face of rivalry refer to the decisions you make based on the information you have. Perhaps you are facing a difficult time or a hard decision. Maybe you are in front of someone who is trying to tell you that their way is better than the way you are considering doing things. Whichever it is, the next move you make will determine the outcome you are going to deal with.

In the previous sections, we touched on the growth mindset as a concept to adopt to make sure you do not allow rivalry to tear you down. Well, this is just as applicable in the face of challenging people. The way you choose to act will affect the outcome you see taking place because certain people are set in your life for the simple reason to put you through trials and tribulations. There are a few things to consider here. For example, the person in front of you may be a rival, but they may also be someone who is pushing you to do something specific because they actually want you to succeed. As such, one of the key questions to be asking yourself is whether the person in your way is indeed there to act as a rival or whether they are there to reconsider your options and to make a decision that is more in your best interest.

Aside from this, there is also a question of timing. While it is true that life may sometimes "just happen," I do believe that some people are set in our path at a time when we can learn a certain lesson from them. For example, you may have people in your life that, through the bad influence they had on you, led you to avoid an even stickier situation later. Perhaps it was someone in your entourage who made you drink or smoke as you were too young to be able to understand the consequences of the choices you were making, or maybe it's someone who pushed you to do something you did not want to do, although you did not know any better. While these experiences are negative ones and

Don't bring much other than negativity and hurt; they can also bring positivity by teaching you valuable lessons. The moves you make at that very moment will determine your outcome. Will you learn a lesson from this bad experience, or will you simply continue a path that brings you nothing but unhappiness? Will you let this person exert control over you by letting rivalry win - by letting them push you to make a decision that is not in your favor, or will you put yourself first and focus on the long-term, more positive consequences?

The perfect example may be one that you can relate to. If you have been working on a big project to achieve certain goals, such as launching a business, finally getting a degree, or something along those lines, you already know the amount of sacrifice you have had to put in. And, if there were no sacrifices along the way, then I envy you! In any case, it is not rare that sacrifice is something along the lines of having to give up a night out with friends to finish up work or take a client/investor's call that could completely change the situation for you. So, what choice would you make if you knew what the outcome was going to be? Would you miss that call to go to the pub with your friends? Would you choose to skip class if you knew that your potential future employer was going to give a guest lecture? Would you choose to smoke and drink when you were young if you knew that it was going to get you surrounded by the wrong crowd?

Sometimes, situations are your biggest rivals. Similarly, the people involved in the situations that are testing you are also there because they push you to question the moves you are making. Is the timing correct? What impact will this decision have on the outcomes you are expecting? Is this the night timing? Life will continue to put you through trials and tribulations, and the people you surround yourself with - and those who come up to you out of the blue when you least expect it-are going to push you to make certain moves. This is crucial to make with the right mindset and with your head on your shoulders. Not doing so might cost you more than you may think.

It's About the People You Hang Around

Are you in the right crowd? Are you surrounded by the right kinds of people, or do you know that you should surround yourself with better people to fit the kind of life you want to establish for yourself? While the moves you make within specific situations affect the outcomes you see and enjoy, there is another key player in the outcomes you will experience: the people you hang around with, the support system you have, how the people around you act, and, most importantly, how they influence you. The people you hang around aren't just your friends or the random colleagues that you see every day. This category of people includes the people who help bring you up and who act as a support system whenever you face adversity or rivalry in your life. They are there to bring positive vibes and more happiness to your life. After all, the saying "your vibe attracts your tribe" isn't so far from the truth. In fact, I'd go as far as to argue that it's 100% accurate!

There are many advantages to having a support system, but it's important to understand that a support system is a two-way street. It doesn't just happen by accident. Healthy support systems are vital to a person's well-being because they provide feedback and support, educate a person about their problems and help them make better decisions. In addition, a supportive social network can help a person achieve their personal goals by pushing them to keep going, even when every fiber in their being tells them to stop.

A support system can offer more than advice. They can also help people discover their passions and pursue their dreams. Having a support system which is what the people you hang around with, should give you a large network of contacts to help you find - your way in the world. This network can also serve as a source of inspiration, which will keep you motivated to meet your goals or to stand tall whenever you face a rival (whether that's a person or a negative situation). A support group can also offer emotional support and deepen your knowledge of yourself, such as what your weaknesses may be, and hence, when you may be getting yourself in a sticky situation because of them. By providing emotional and social support, the people you hang around with can be invaluable. On the other hand, if the group of people you are surrounded by pulls you down (whether you realize it or not at the time), you need to get rid of it.

A support system can help a person feel more confident and capable. When you're under stress, you can begin to question your abilities and start seeing your weaknesses instead of your strengths. A good support network can give you a boost when you're facing a challenging situation and remind you of your strengths. Your group of friends or even just acquaintances can also be a buffer against the negative effects of stress, such as those that make you make bad decisions or some that may feel good now but which you may regret later on.

If you're not around someone you trust, you may be susceptible to developing self-doubt.

On the other hand, if you trust the wrong crowd, you may be entering the beginning stage of downfall into negativity and something that makes you bow down to rivalry. If you let others make you feel like you are less than you are or if you let them, make you question yourself - you are more likely to give in to temptations such as giving up on a dream or something that may seem trivial, such as skipping a meeting that could potentially be life-changing (as was discussed in the previous section).

There's another side to this coin, however, which is that the people you hang around with can also work as a team to bring you up. Of course, this is not meant to sound as though everyone's life revolves around helping you up, but rather as though you can be a part of this team and hence can bring them up too. A team is just that: a group of people that

Pushes each other up. Ultimately, kingdoms did not fall to one person, but it took a team with a common cause. You can build anything as long as you have a vision, and people will follow! So, why put yourself in a team that brings itself down? Why surround yourself with cancerous people that act as parasites and just make you worse off?

Similarly, the family you have is the one group of people who is likely to be there, no matter what happens. While it's true that you may not always have them around, especially if you come from a background that isn't the strongest in terms of family ties - you can still most count on your family to be there for you as an unconditional support system. If your family isn't present, you need to surround yourself with people who will be there for you when you most need them. We touched on friends as a support system and especially as a team that works in your favor, but your family is also likely to always be there.

Having a strong family is beneficial for many reasons. Not only does it make you feel less alone, but it can also improve your mental health. Having a strong family around you can alleviate some of the stress that you might be experiencing as it provides a solid foundation and people to fall back on if things don't work out. A strong family is a community of people that you can lean on when you're facing tough situations. It can help you overcome anxiety and fear. It can also help you overcome obstacles and make you feel more confident and resilient when you feel like the world is against you. It will encourage you to reach your goals and achieve success and will help you gain that mental toughness and self-worth when you feel like you can't overcome an obstacle because family is unconditional - you don't choose it!

CHAPTER FIVE

CANCEROUS PEOPLE (SNAKES)

As you have read so far, it's not rare that we end up surrounding ourselves with the wrong kinds of crowds. Sometimes, we just end up with people next to us that make us think, what the hell am I doing here? I can tell you that I've had situations like these. For example, I went to a party last summer where I ended up surrounded by people who were just complaining about their situation non-stop. In the meantime, they weren't ready to do anything about it. Instead, they preferred to stand there and complain endlessly about the system, the government, their financial situation, and so on. And then, as I would bring up a point of reflection or challenge their view, I would see all eyes on me, some of them smirking, and would be either dismissed or ridiculed. Otherwise, they would simply tell me I was too idealistic instead of questioning where I was coming from or where I was basing my information on. While it's okay to have disagreements with people, it isn't as okay to feel like whenever you are bringing up a point or perspective; you are dismissed or ridiculed. Similarly, if you feel like your happiness, engagement, or your light, in general, is tamed down, then it's time to act and change the circumstances you are in.

Being able to identify cancerous people is tough, so you must watch and understand their patterns to start recognizing the tactics that they use. It is often more than just a disagreement of ideas, but one's pure purpose is to see you fall. Indeed, cancerous people don't want to see you happy, nor do they want you to succeed. They may say that they do, but they usually say so to then fraternize with you just to pull you down the second they can. Some people don't even know they're cancerous because they're so used to being in that state of mind that the very sight of your light threatens them and their darkness. You must be able to spot these patterns and move on from them.

Sadly, it could be someone you love. It could be a roommate, your partner, family members; you name it. For example, there are people who are purposely nice to some people, showing a nice smile and being only positive, only to turn around and absolutely tear the person apart behind their back. Similarly, in many cases, a person's misfortune is the other's source of contentment. As such, you need to be careful about the kind of people you surround yourself with, and you must be able to spot the signs of toxicity.

Toxic Relationships: The Perfect Example of a Cancerous Person

In a toxic relationship, you may find yourself being constantly threatened, coerced, and otherwise pushed down. Such behavior is never acceptable, and the person responsible for the abuse may make you think you're crazy if you feel that way - this is called gaslighting. Toxic relationships can cause you to lose your self-worth, confidence, and

Self-esteem. They can also affect your future. Keeping a toxic relationship is detrimental to your health, so you should work on spotting the signs of this toxicity. If you're in a relationship with someone who is toxic, it's best to get help as soon as possible - especially if it is a personal relationship, such as with a partner. By taking action now, you can prevent the consequences and start living a healthier life.

Nonetheless, cancerous people can be found just about anywhere. A cancerous person may simply be someone who cannot wait to see you fall and fail, or it may be a classmate who gives you the wrong kind of information just because he or she wants to see you fall down and get worse grades. Otherwise, it may also be a family member who constantly brings you down or even just a friend who won't stop putting your negativity down and who, instead, just pushes more negativity into your life. Perhaps you are trying extremely hard to remain positive, to only use appropriate language, and to focus on what's going well in your life. And yet, you're stuck with this person who keeps on trying to put your light out. Stay away from them. Follow your intuition. If there's something telling you that this person is not your friend or does not want your best, stay away. Keep your distance, and if you can't, do your best to only allow them to see certain parts of you. Don't give them more power than they should have - trust me; they'll use every ounce of it they can to limit you!

Projecting: Are You Teaching or Forcing Your Own Beliefs on Others?

When we aim to talk to others about things that matter to us, we usually do so with positive intentions. We want to teach others about their actions, how they may be negatively affecting us, and hence, why we would like them to stop. However, there is a difference between teaching and forcing our own beliefs on others. If we believe that a certain way of acting is wrong, it may be true and non-negotiable to us, but it may simply not be a part of the other person's reality. For example, you may feel that showing up 5 minutes late is rude and disrespectful of the other person's time. On the other hand, the person you are telling this to may feel that 5 minutes is not considered late and that as long as they warn others, there is no real issue. In a different scenario, if you feel angry because many people had shown up late when you were meant to meet them and let out all your aggressivity and anger on them, you may be projecting rather than sharing your opinion. Be careful with this: while you may have beliefs, don't make the mistake of forcing them onto others. Sometimes, we project our feelings onto others and give them bad intentions when it’s a problem that we need to deal with internally instead.

Be aware of this: you can be cancer to yourself by trying to seek the approval of others. That's a hole you're digging without an end. No one will care for your time more than YOU will. They could love you, but at the end of the day, a decade can pass by when you realize you did what was comfortable for them and not comfortable for YOU. Know when to make your boundaries clear- such as showing up on time - and when to adjust

To what may be a belief and yet not something that can be expected of everyone. If you cannot adjust or adapt, then your boundaries come into place. This is where you must decide: do you stick around, or do you put yourself first?

CHAPTER SIX

IDENTITY

When thinking about escaping cancerous people, you may be wondering, okay, cool, but how do I do that? By being 100% clear on who you are. Sounds simplistic? Because it is. When you are solid on your two feet and know exactly what you stand for or against, you are also in a much better position to know what you agree with, disagree with, what you think is right or wrong, and how you like to be treated. For this, you need to understand what makes you happy, sad, what you think is right or wrong (your principles), and what you believe in. And then, you need to know how to separate belief from fact so as to know when you may need to take a step back from the rival in front of you to better understand their position. While your beliefs may feel like they are foolproof and 100% accurate, they are only those beliefs. As such, you need to be strong and know your principles to stand up to a rival, but you also must know when to back down and choose whether the battle ahead is one worth finding. As such, when faced with a challenge, bring yourself back to this: who am I? What are my beliefs? What is my identity composed of?

Your identity is a combination of your expressions, beliefs, looks, qualities, and personality. How does your identity come to be? What has made you who you are? And what does this have to do with your self-esteem? What are your favorite things to do? What are your hobbies? What are your favorite movies? Who do you look up to? These all influence your identity or your sense of self. An individual's identity is an array of traits, expressions, looks, and qualities that make them who they are. It is an essential part of our understanding of who we are. Our identity is often at the heart of our individuality. It is more than a combination of features; it is a complete persona that defines us and gives us meaning. It influences how we see ourselves, the world around us, and hence, it influences the actions that we take. We can also use our identity to our advantage. It can define the things we like, what we don't like, and how we view ourselves when we face a rival and need to stand up to them. If we feel good about ourselves and have a sense of purpose, then we have achieved it - we know who we are and what our identity is composed of. The most important part of our identity is our sense of self-worth and the values we hold dear.

Our identity is a multidimensional construct that encompasses many aspects of who we are. It includes the physical traits, such as eye color, fingerprint, or how we look, as well as our behavioral traits. These attributes are combined to make us unique. This allows us to be recognized by others and to distinguish ourselves from others. Developing a sense of self is an important aspect of identity, and we can make use of it to help ourselves better understand why we may react a certain way during a situation and why others may be able to handle it better. For example, if you find yourself often struggling to have debates without raising your voice and losing your cool, it may be because you feel like your opinions are not valued. As such, this is part of your identity. A lack of self-confidence or self-worth - may be the cause of this behavior. Once you know this, you can also act on it.

Our identity is the way we present ourselves to the world. We can be born with a certain identity, or it can be influenced by what others think of us. In a society that is based on power and status, our identity can sometimes be confused with what we present to the world in this regard. Your idea of your social status and sense of self-value can affect your identity, too, as you try and emulate the person you would like others to think you are, hence why we tend to do things that we may not agree with if we think that others will look up to us more as we do them.

Our identity is our personality, passions, and interests. It helps us achieve our potential. It can be a positive or negative trait. Whatever defines us is what makes us unique. Those traits are our strengths and can help define ourselves when we face adversity - even if there is a rival, we can stand strong and know who we are and hence what we think is right or wrong. A positive self-image will help you live your life to the fullest as it helps you think, "cool, this person's opinion is irrelevant anyway because I know where I stand on this matter." Of course, remember that constructive criticism is valuable too! If you're happy with who you are, the world will see you as you are happy. That alone is a great way to get yourself past challenges.

CHAPTER SEVEN

YOU CAN'T WIN THEM ALL – LIVE AND LEARN!

When we think about our rivals, we may also think about the people that have been doing better than us. It's difficult on the ego when we realize that others have been playing the game better than we have. After all, we all want to succeed, and we want to be the best at what we do. Being able to learn that sometimes, we can't win them all is a big lesson to learn, but it's also a crucial one to integrate into our mindset. It's okay to want to be the best, but if you do not accept that you can't be the best at everything, you're in for a rough awakening

Life is full of hurdles and challenges, and it's something that we need to accept. When we have a rival facing us, whether it's a person or a situation that we are conflicted by, we need to realize that it's okay to fail. There is no fun, no motivation, and no incentive to try hard and to keep going if all that we do ends up being perfect. Similarly, if we only set ourselves up for success and never accept any failure, it may turn against our favor - if the fear of failing and of seeing our rival win is petrifying, we may simply end up lowering the expectations we have for ourselves. Thus, accept that you may not win them all. There will be times where others will be better than you at something. There will be situations where there is truly no exit route but only one possibility - failing or accepting that the reality is not the ideal one we had envisioned. Once you accept this, you avoid the negative and dangerous pitfall that is limiting yourself to only what you know is possible and what you know you will succeed at. No growth has ever been seen or achieved when only remaining in one's comfort zone.

Speaking of growth, that is another lesson to consider in regard to losing a certain game or failing in the face of a rival. When you don't win, you have two options: to wallow in your sadness and disappointment or to take the opportunity that you must learn from the experience and grow from the lessons you have learned. Being able to learn from the experience is a skill, and perhaps to your surprise, it is one that not many can take advantage of. You may think that it is common for people to sit down, consider what has just happened, and to learn from experience by consciously asking themselves what could be done better next time. Unfortunately, it's not the case! Many simple take the loss and either let themselves be stopped by it, give in to the negativity and stop progressing, or they end up repeating the same mistakes again, only to end up being considerably more frustrated with the situation than they previously were. This, you can avoid. You must learn, and you must grow, and for that, you must be able to accept when things don't go as well as you'd want them to.

Ultimately, you cannot win at everything you do. If you are currently thinking, well, I'm pretty successful, and I can't think of the last time I didn't win or ended up failing..., then I have some news for you: you need to push yourself further. Your comfort zone is called such for a reason - it's comfortable, it's well-known, and it's something you know how to handle. The real challenge here is to force yourself to get out of it. That's the only way you'll grow, and it's the best way to learn. Make mistakes, learn from them, and see how it affects your growth. It's worth it!

CHAPTER EIGHT

MATCHING VIBRATIONAL ENERGY

I have always been interested in the Law of Attraction but always found there was something missing with it. It's only in the last 5 months that I believe I have found out what's missing, and the results of my own experimentation have been amazing. This is where matching vibrational energy comes in.

I've been experimenting for a few months now, and I'd like to share it with you today.

Other Peoples Energy

Whilst standing in a queue at the bank, I felt strong vibes from a woman in front of me. She was extremely impatient, sighing and tutting as she wasn't getting attended to quickly enough. There were only two tellers on at the time, and there were about 6 people in front of us. I could feel that she was getting more and more frustrated and angry and could almost physically feel the vibes she was sending out.

She eventually turned around to me, hoping to get me in the same state, and said, 'you'd think they put on more clerks at the till.' I smiled politely and looked straight ahead. A few minutes went by, and she turned around again and said, 'I mean, it's lunchtime; you'd think they would know it's going to be busy.' Now, I hate being around people like this, so I said, 'What can you do about it?' She gave me a funny look: 'What do you mean?' she replied, 'Well, you're wasting all this energy getting annoyed, but it's not going to make the queue go down any quicker, is it?'

When she realized I didn't feel the same, she turned and waited in line quitely, but probably seething inside.

We all know people like this in our lives. People that give off these vibes of anger, negativity, boredom, un-satisfaction. The thing is, they don't need to say anything most of the time. We can actually feel it inside us.

We also know people who are radiant, and as soon as they walk into a room, there is a hoard of people attracted to them.

It's the same when we walk into a restaurant, a nightclub, a party at a house; we immediately get this 'vibe' about the place. Why is that, and what is it telling us?

When you get a 'vibe' about something, you are really saying, 'I am feeling a vibrational energy inside of me.' think about it for a second; that's exactly what a vibe is. You can't touch it, smell it, see it, hear it or taste it; you FEEL it.

So if we presume that a vibe is vibrational energy, and it's this energy that causes a reaction in us to FEEL something, you, therefore, have to presume that vibrational energy is real, although unseen, and causes a reaction inside of us.

If someone else, or a place, can cause a reaction inside of us with its vibrational energy, wouldn't it be a good idea to play around, with a sense of curiosity and excitement, with the idea that we can project our energy, and even match the energy of a similar nature and pull it toward us to get the things we want in life?

Matching Vibrations

Have you ever tried to tune a guitar by ear?

What you have to do is pluck the 1st string (maybe tune it first), then on the second string, hold the fifth fret down and pluck the string so it matches the sound of the open first string.

Basically, what you are doing is matching the vibration of the first string to the vibration of the second string, and you do this with all six strings until the guitar is tuned.

Just like a magnet, we have repelled away from people who do not have similar vibrational energy as us. For example, can you think of a time when you were in a great mood, happy, and loving life? You got to work with the same energy and come across someone who is on a real downer. Three things can happen in this situation:

1. You avoid them like the plague as they will sap that energy straight from you.

2. You lend some of your vibrational energy to the other person to pick them up; however you can only do this for so long, as your energy will be gone before long.

3. They avoid you like the plague as you are too damn happy for them.

Matching vibrational energy helps our body/mind seek out vibrations of a similar nature. I believe this is how we get the things we want in our lives, and I've been playing around with this idea for months now with some great results.

How to match vibrations

There are lots of ways to match your internal vibrations with the things you want in life:

- **Visualization –** We all know this one and may have tried it, but there's a trick to this which I'll share in a moment.

- **Writing –** write down what you want to have in your life

- **Belief working –** work on your beliefs about why you have not got what you want in your life. There are sometimes, or a lot of times, when you have a limiting belief stopping you from matching vibrations to the thing you want.

There are a lot of other ways, but with all of them, there is a huge factor missed out when the likes of 'The Secret' and 'LOA' authors speak about it, and that is: FEELING.

When the authors of 'the Secret' spoke about using our thoughts to attract the things we want in life, they were only giving you an introduction to the subject.

What has been missing is that you do indeed use your thoughts, but it's not your thoughts that have the power; it's the feeling you get when you have these thoughts. But, you have to keep using your thoughts to get that deep feeling inside you, 'The Vibe.' When you have 'the Vibe,' then you know you are matching your vibrational energy and aligning it with the object of your desire, whether it be money, a new job, a new person in your life, or whatever it is you want.

When you get that vibe, your body becomes radiant, and, I believe, there are no boundaries to the distance of your radiance.

Charging Your Vibrational Energy

What I have found is that 'the Vibe' needs to be charged. It's no good getting your vibe charged up only to let the charge run down; you have to keep charging it up with whatever method you choose to charge it: visualization, writing, talking, etc.

One word of advice. I wouldn't use affirmations for matching vibrations. However, affirmations are an amazing way to change your underlying beliefs about not charging your vibrational state

Another thing I have learned from my experiments is that desperation causes you to lose the very thing you desire in your life.

For example, if you want more money in your life, and all you think about is money, you obsess about it and get more frustrated as the more you think about it, the less of it you get. You're holding on too tight. What you should be obsessing about is the process and the service you give to others.

How it has helped me!

I've just finished my accounts for my online business for the last financial year, April 2020 "April 2021. I managed to get around $1500 per month directly from sales of my books, courses, blog advertising, etc. However, I also managed to spend around $1300 per month on advertising, new programs, new software, courses, coaching, affiliate payments, etc. I was so involved in lots of different programs to make more money than I lost track of why I was doing it. It's not just about the money; it is about serving others and teaching what I have learned myself. When I started to focus on the question: "˜How can I better serve my subscribers and the readers of the blog?' My income shot up.

This year to date, I have April 2021 "August 2021, I have a net profit of around $2000 per month, and gross sales of around $4,000 per month, with $2000 being spent on servers, email accounts, coaching, affiliates, designers, etc. I still have a full-time job, so the figure could be much better.

Sales of How to Become an Advanced Early Riser account for 25% of the net profit, which is great as it wasn't really selling at the beginning. Word of mouth and relationship marketing alone has increased the sales more and more each month

I had a limiting belief about my income, believing that if I could reach $1,000 per month online, I would be happy, but I didn't re-calibrate this belief, and sales were stuck at that ceiling when I reached it. When I re-calibrated back in February/March, sales started coming in thick and fast.

I also had a lack of urgency. As I have a full-time job, there is no immediate urgency to do as well online; when I pushed myself to set target dates, coupled with getting rid of the limiting beliefs, focus, energy, and income shot up.

My feeling now is to net over $10,000 per month with gross sales reaching $12,500 per month

This is purely down to realizing why I write, why I do what I do, and focusing my actions on better serving readers, subscribers, and advertisers on the blog. I also look at my beliefs about what I am doing and re-calibrate my vibrational energy to match what I want and how best to help others.

Protect Yourself Against Energy Vampires

We all know at least one energy vampire. They might be perfectly nice; in fact, they generally are, but spending time with them leaves you feeling drained and weak. They complain to you about their lives; you commiserate with them. You do want to help them feel better, and they often do after speaking with you. But at what cost? Is there a way to deal with these energy vampires other than cutting them out of your life altogether? How can you protect yourself against other people "robbing" you of your energy?

First of all, it's important to understand exactly what is happening on an energetic level. No one can "rob" you of your energy. Your energy is not finite, and you can't give it away or take it from someone else. Energy vampirism generally comes about when someone with a lower vibration seeks out someone with a higher vibration and uses them to raise their own vibration a bit - making them feel better in the process. The issue arises when the person with the higher vibration isn't stable in that frequently and allows the person with the lower vibration to influence them energetically.

If you're a person who's often been accused of being overly sensitive or empathetic, you're probably someone who is easily influenced by the energy around you. Don't worry; this doesn't mean that you're broken somehow. It just means that you never learned how to stabilize your vibration. And how could you have? The answer isn't to "just deal with it" or "grow up," as you might've been told. But it also means that you don't have to be at the mercy of the frequencies around you. You can definitely learn to hold your vibration, even when faced with an energy vampire.

If you're often sought out by others to make them feel better, the chances are that your vibration is probably generally on the high side. You may allow yourself to be influenced, but you always eventually return to your naturally high vibration. You're probably quite positive and loving, and others naturally feel-good energy flowing off you. Again, this isn't a bad thing - you're a natural uplifter - unless, of course, you're faced with someone who begins to pull your vibration down.

Let's say that someone you care about is upset and wants to talk to you about it. Fair enough. You're a caring person; you love to help. This friend of yours begins to complain about her boss and what a jerk he is. Her work life is nothing but stress. She goes on and on about how horrible her colleagues are, the backstabbing that goes on, how depressing it all is, and how she feels utterly helpless in her situation. And what do you do? You listen intently, make soothing comments, and you begin to empathize. You begin to put yourself in her shoes. You imagine what it must be like for her. That's what good friends do, right? You see how hopeless the situation is. Even if you come up with some solutions, she's quick to point out why they won't work. You begin to feel what she feels. You are lowering your vibration to match hers.

It's important to note that this has nothing to do with her. She cannot force you to lower your vibration. No one can. You have to let it happen. Not letting it happen is, of course, much easier when you're consciously aware of what's going on. So, now that you know what's happening on an energetic level, what can you do the next time your friend comes around to complain?

One solution, of course, is to just stop talking to her. Now, generally, this isn't a great option since it won't always be possible to get away from lower frequency people, and learning how to stabilize your vibration will protect you in all situations. However, sometimes you need to get away from the energy drain for a bit in order to stabilize. This applies to geographic locations as well. You might have a hard time stabilizing your vibration in a certain city or country, for example, or you might not be strong enough to raise your vibration while in a certain job. It's entirely possible to return to that location or company at a later time, once you're stronger, and not be affected by it anymore.

Let's assume that cutting your friend out of your life is not really an option. Here's what I advise: Refuse to play in her playground with her. You are going to consciously hold on to your good feeling vibration. And if she wants to play with you in your higher, yummy, optimistic playground, then she has to join you where you are. You're not going to come to her playground of misery and despair. Make no mistake - this will take discipline. And if your friend is used to you commiserating with her, she will most likely react badly to the change at first. Persevere. This does not mean that you have to be fake-happy. Just be who you are and stay there.

Here are some options:

- Change the subject. When she begins to complain about her boss, tell her that you'd really like to talk about something else. You know that she really wants to feel better, and you think that it'll be much easier to accomplish that if you both focus on a happy subject. Explain that beating the drum of how horrible her job is just ended up making you both feel bad.

- Keep turning the subject around. If she talks about her jerk of a boss, ask her if he's always a jerk or just sometimes. Does he have any redeeming qualities at all? Try to get her to focus on that. Yes, this will annoy her at first. She wants to complain to you, and she wants you to join her so she can feel validated. But you're going to refuse to join her - for your sake. Remember that she's used to you lowering your vibration to meet hers. If you suddenly refuse, she will either need to raise her vibration to meet yours or get away from you. The vibrational discord between you will be too uncomfortable. You have to become a match or split. And if you refuse to budge, she will have to. Or she'll walk away. If that's the case, let it happen.

- Do not see your friend as helpless and stuck. She is not. She may currently think that she is, but she's just as powerful a being as you are. And you cannot force her to realize it any more than she can force you to lower your vibration. But know that when you do lower your energy to match hers - you are in no way helping her. The only true way to help her is to keep holding your vibration and give her the chance to come up and meet you.

- Find something YOU can feel good about in the conversation and focus on it. You are not actively trying to get her to raise her vibration. That's not your job. Your goal is to stay where you are. So even if you listen to her saga, translate all of it into a perspective that you can feel good about.

- Walk away. If the situation becomes too uncomfortable for you (neither one of you is budging), make an excuse and walk away. You are not abandoning her. If she can't hear you, can't come up to meet your vibration, and you know that you cannot help her by lowering your vibration, then you have to take a break. This may well happen the first couple of times. Remember that she is used to you behaving one way and probably won't react well to the sudden change. But you can't help anyone from a place of low vibration, so protecting your own frequency has to come first.

Practice this technique with strangers at first - it will be most difficult to use with people you care a great deal about. You don't have to become cold or uncaring; you don't have to become hostile or fake happiness. You can still be loving and compassionate (more so, in fact, when your vibration stays high), you can still help people. Just refuse to let others determine how you feel.

This will take a bit of work. It might even take a lifetime to learn how to hold your vibration in ALL situations. Even people who have incredibly stable vibrations would have a hard time walking into a warzone and staying happy and at peace. This is why you shouldn't be afraid to remove yourself from a situation that makes it impossible for you to stabilize. The rest, however, can be conquered with a bit of perseverance and practice. Good luck!

CHAPTER NINE

CHANGE YOUR BELIEFS

If you are struggling with negative beliefs, the solution for you may be as simple as taking a course on how to do what you believe you can't. Sometimes a little education can change your understanding enough that what once seemed impossible is now more believable for you. Look up courses at your local college, or ask others how they did it. If you want to start a business but don't think you can do it, take some business courses online or at night at your local college, and ask other business owners how they got started. Then take what you learn and put it into action. Knowledge is power, but it's only latent power until you put action behind it. A little extra knowledge may be all you need to shift your beliefs.

When we hold negative beliefs, they're often based on a story we tell ourselves. We can't do this or that because...(you fill in the blank). One way to address this is to use affirmations. Here's an exercise you can do. Write down what it is you want to be, do, or have. Then write down all the reasons you believe you can't. Now, the opposite of why you can't probably be what you need to believe in achieving what you desire. Make a list of these opposites. With this list of positive beliefs, generate affirmative statements like "I have all the skills I need to do X" or "I am worth five hundred dollars a day."

Now that you have a list of positive affirmations spend a couple of minutes several times throughout the day repeating these statements to yourself. It's best if you can do it out loud while looking at yourself in the mirror. Try also doing it first thing in the morning when you wake up and at night just before you fall asleep. This is when your subconscious mind is most open to new ideas since your conscious mind isn't as alert and isn't applying the same level of resistance to what you're saying.

At first, what you're saying will seem like a lie, but keep at it. Over time, the repetition will begin to influence your subconscious mind, and your beliefs will begin to shift toward what you are telling yourself.

Visualization

Visualization is similar to affirmations, except that you're using images instead of words and phrases. The best way to explain visualization is through an example. Let's say you want to lose 25 pounds, but you believe you'll never be able to do it. Take some quiet time for yourself when you won't be disturbed - again, the best time to do this is first thing in the morning upon waking or just before falling asleep at night, since this is when your subconscious mind is most open to the influence. Close your eyes and picture what you would look like after having lost 25 pounds. See how happy you are, see others congratulating you on losing that weight. After watching yourself for a while, merge into that version of you that you're observing; be the you that you're watching. See your new self with your own eyes, feel what it's like to be slim, look at yourself in a mirror and admire yourself, hear others congratulating you and telling you how great you look. Totally and completely be that slimmer you.

If you make this visualization a daily practice, your subconscious mind will begin to hold onto that image of you being slim and will begin to exert influence on your daily thoughts and actions to help you change your current reality to match the new image of you. In other words, your subconscious mind will "make" you take action to lose weight; it can't allow there to be a conflict between what it believes and what the external reality is. Your weight loss will no longer feel like a battle that can't be won; instead, it will seem effortless because you won't even be consciously doing anything. All the actions will result from an unconscious influence.

You can take this same approach with anything you would like to change. Do you want to be healthier? Visualize yourself healthy. Do you want to have more money? Visualize yourself making the income you desire; picture the cheques coming in, making the bank deposits, spending the money. Want to be more outgoing and have more friends? Visualize it. The daily visualization time will transform the limiting beliefs that are preventing you from achieving.

Mastermind groups

If you really want to change your beliefs, start hanging around people who have already done or are doing what you wish you could. Most of us have heard the term "birds of a feather flock together." Generally, this is quite true. The wealthy tend to hang out with other wealthy people. Athletic people tend to hang out with other athletic people, intellectuals hang around other intellectual people, and so on. How can you use this to change your beliefs? Hang out with people who are doing or have what you want, and your beliefs will start shifting to match theirs. Here's a little test you can take to verify this. Take stock of the people you hang out with: Do most of their incomes come within 20% plus or minus what you make? There are probably some exceptions, but for the most part, people find this to be true. What do you think would happen if you started hanging out with people who are making the income you desire to make? The group mentality idea is quite true; use it to your advantage. You can learn a lot from others who are where you would like to be, and you will pick up on their energy and belief systems. Not only that, but you will directly witness that what you desire is not unachievable.

Subliminal and hypnosis technology

This method is pretty straightforward. You can use audio, video, or professional services to obtain subliminal or hypnotic services.

Subliminal technology is often either music or videos with embedded messages your conscious mind doesn't see or hear, but your subconscious mind is able to pick them up. This method is able to send the messages directly to your subconscious mind, bypassing the assessment of the conscious mind. With repeated use, these messages will begin to shape the beliefs of the subconscious. Some subliminal software also uses audio technology that entrains the frequency at which the brain is operating to a lower level, which can help the subliminal messages to better penetrate. Just a word of warning with this: please be sure to read the instructions carefully before use. If the product you're using utilizes entrainment technology, you should not do any activities that require alertness while listening. I personally find the best time to use these products is when I go to bed. I set them to loop continuously; it helps me fall asleep, and I continue to get the subliminal messages even while I'm sleeping.

Hypnosis is possible through professional services or with pre-recorded audio tracks. Hypnosis guides you to a deeply relaxed state and then submits positive messages to your brain. In this deeply relaxed state, the mind is more receptive to the messages being sent. If you're using pre-recorded audio, you'll need to set aside some quiet time for yourself each day to use this technology.

Letting Go

What you resist persists. The more you resist your negative beliefs, the more they will be reinforced. This is something I've always struggled with on my self-improvement journey. It's hard not to resist the negative stuff you want to change. However, the more attention you give these negative things, the more they will continue to impact your life in a negative way. The goal is to desire to change, but at the same time to accept yourself the way you are now. Try to keep your attention on having or being what you want instead of focusing on the things that are wrong with you now. One way you can help yourself do this is to first take some time to give your negative thoughts and emotions some attention. This might sound strange but stay with me for a minute. If instead of resisting the thing you want to change, just stop for a few minutes and allow yourself to really just feel that negative thought or emotion. Just allow it to be without fighting it. After a while, you'll find that the feeling will reduce or totally dissolve. Each time it comes up, just allow yourself to feel it again without fighting it. Each time you do this, you're letting go of it just a little bit more until eventually it's gone.

What we're doing with this method is just allowing the negativity to be. We spend so much time fighting or resisting what we want to change that we never just allow it to be, to exist—taking time to simply allow our negative thoughts and feelings to give our body and brain time to process and experience them. As you process these things, they begin to let go on their own. As they let go, you'll find that the energy and focus you had been using to resist them becomes free, and you can then redirect this energy toward positive change instead of resisting negativity in your life.

Meditation

Meditation is usually a more spiritually focused practice, but it is useful in many ways. It can infuse you with the traits of the Universe (or God, or whatever term you use to describe the "higher power"). There is no lack; there is no "can't"; there are only pure choices to make without any limitations. The Universe does not try to do something; it has no doubts. Meditation connects you to the Source of all there is. As that connection builds, you will find that your limiting beliefs and thoughts begin to dissolve, and eventually, you can achieve a full conscious connection (enlightenment). You'll begin to see challenges and limitations in life as opportunities to learn and grow instead of obstacles that hold you back. You will be more at peace, and you will begin to flow with life instead of feeling as though you're trying to swim upstream. On a simpler level, meditation allows you to empty the mind, slow down, relax, take time for yourself. This in itself is beneficial and is also good for focus and self-discovery. There are many different meditation forms and techniques. Experiment with different ones until you find a few you like. Many cities now have meditation groups you could join. There are also many guided meditation CDs and lots of websites that offer meditation exercises you can try.

As with most anything in life, do not expect instant results with these techniques and give up after trying something for a few days without results. In most cases, it takes at least 3 weeks to begin to make shifts in behaviors and beliefs, so pick one or more of the above methods and commit to your betterment by doing them for at least twenty-one days straight. If you miss a day, don't get down on yourself; just try to refocus and start over again. After twenty-one days, you should be able to determine how well a particular method is working for you. Even after three weeks, your life may not have made a dramatic shift, but pay attention to comments other people may be making about you. Often others can see changes in you before you become aware of them yourself.

CHAPTER TEN

KEEP PUSHING

So, you now know that you cannot win them all. No matter what you have been working on achieving, you are facing people who are continuously testing you, people who will be making you doubt yourself, and of course, you will be facing difficult times that will test your very own resilience too. Therefore, once you learn that you can't win all fights and can't get everyone to like you, you need to simply keep pushing. In life, you will have tough times. That's inevitable. However, the real difference is made when you can show solid resilience.

What is resilience? As a baseline, we understand it as the ability to overcome challenges without letting ourselves fall and stay down. Resilience is a complex trait that can be learned and developed. It's not an inherited trait but the result of an array of internal and external factors, including your mental health, lived experiences, and many more. Another critical variable is social support, which can be cultivated throughout your years on this planet and, therefore, the extent to which you feel like you have the support of those around you. Resilient people believe they have control over their lives and tend not to blame others for their problems. They also have an internal locus of control, meaning that they know where to go to find control over their situation. Thus, when they face tough times, they know how to ground themselves and re-gain control over the circumstances they find themselves in.

Individuals with high levels of resilience may possess a strong moral compass, beliefs, cognitive and emotional flexibility, and a sense of social connectedness. They do not dwell on negative experiences, seeking instead to find meaning and purpose in life's trials and tribulations. They might begin a meditation practice, take an online course, or learn how to play the guitar when they feel like they are missing a sense of purpose. These individuals indeed also have a strong sense of meaning in their lives, such as being a dependable colleague or may aspire to progress in their careers. Ultimately, with resilience, you know when and how to control yourself, and you can gauge when you need to spend some time working on yourself. You keep pushing because you are motivated to do so by yourself.

Resilience requires a strong sense of character. It enables a person to make responsible choices and to be self-aware. In addition, a strong sense of purpose motivates people to work hard and make a positive contribution to their community, which is something that may help you feel like you can keep pushing, even when you face tough times. These traits make a person like you more resilient and prepared to deal with adversity. Resilience is an individual's capacity to recover from adversity and develop new skills for coping. As such, it's exactly what you need if you're struggling to see where you are going next - to build this resilience and to internalize that whatever struggle you may face, you can always overcome it. So, keep pushing. Know who you are; stand strong and tall on your own two feet. Get back up and strive for the best. Don't let life's adversity become your rival - get back up and try again.

CHAPTER ELEVEN

ADAPT TO YOUR REALITY

In previous chapters, we discussed how learning from hard situations and failing in the face of rivalry may be a difficult step for the ego but still remains a crucial step, nonetheless. This skill is not only one where you learn and grow from difficult situations, but it equally requires you to be able to adapt to the reality that you are living in - namely, the reality that the situation you are in is less than ideal Adaptability is one of the most crucial skills any person can have as it allows them to be significantly more resilient than about 90% of others - if you can adapt and adjust to any situation or obstacle, you can already feel comfortable in the fact that any challenge set your way will only act as a hurdle, and not a mountain that is impossible to climb. Having discussed resilience in the previous chapter, you should already be well-acquainted with the idea. Now, however, we're moving our focus to the part of resilience that has to do with your personal ability to accept the things you cannot change, and instead, to change your own ways accordingly so as to limit the damage that is caused.

Can you recall a situation that you were in previously where you truly felt you had no way out? I know some people who are not religious at all and yet, end up praying to a God to help them through such situations when they have absolutely no idea of how they could get themselves out of it. While this may be argued to be a way to cope with a problem, it is not one that provides concrete solutions - sure, you can have hope and faith, but knowing that you will overcome any situation or difficult obstacle is much more comforting.

In order to overcome anything, you must learn to adjust. This may mean modifying yourself if you aren't happy where you are. For example, you may be unhappy with the way you look - the only way to change this is to adapt yourself to your reality by changing the reality - making changes to yourself, so you start liking yourself more. This may mean working on yourself mentally to achieve this. On the other hand, you may also need to adapt yourself to the people you are surrounded by. For example, if you have an important meeting with people who are considering giving you funding for a business idea you have, you may need to adapt your language and your discourse to fit what they want to hear from you. While many are quick to say "just be yourself," in many cases, being ourselves is not enough if we want something dearly. If the person offering to fund has questionable political beliefs, but you need the funding to make it further in your business, you may choose to adapt yourself to the situation while remaining true to yourself inside, knowing that you are willing to take this leap and to make the best of the money you are receiving while accepting that this is a needed sacrifice to further your own goals and growth. It's not selfish or inauthentic - it's simply called adapting to your reality and adjusting to the situation you have at hand.

This can be discussed on a greater scale too! Adjustments can prepare us from the worst while they can protect us from others and ourselves. For example, the Covid-19 crisis pushed us to adapt to new realities and to a complete paradigm shift in the way we see work and life; in general, We adapted to this situation that had sizable consequences globally. This is what it means to adapt to life-you, adjust to the situation, and adjust based on this. That's the only way to overcome anything in life - you need to be able to adjust, adapt, and do what it takes to get past the challenge.

CHAPTER TWELVE

CREATE THE WORLD YOU WANT TO LIVE IN

For our final chapter, we are moving towards the legacy you are leaving behind and the vision you have. Life can be an obstacle course, but once you've eliminated any self-doubt, you must go with the tide and not against it and build a culture where everyone can thrive. Only then can you see the stars align before your very eyes. Therefore, the only rival left is time itself. The legacy you leave behind is something you can look back on later in life. It is something that you work towards, and as such, it is often incorporated as part of your vision. It is something you can look forward to and work on every day.

There are two things to consider when considering leaving a legacy: the type of legacy that you want and your personal values. A legacy that you create must be long-lasting, which means that it must have a life beyond your own time on earth. Your legacy can start before, however, for example, if you were to create a business that was to change the way we live. To create a lasting impact on others, you must passionately immerse your whole self into life and embrace your individuality. Your personal legacy will make a difference, and it will be cherished by future generations.

A legacy is more than just what you leave behind. This means that you will not only leave a lasting impression on other people but also have a positive impact on their lives, enough so that they remember you as the person who provided just this. You can leave a lasting legacy by being generous and kind to those around you, for example, whether this is done directly or indirectly. If you want your legacy to be meaningful, you'll have to show people that you are genuinely excited about the path you are on and the vision you are taking. This is where rivalry comes in: it shapes the legacy you want to leave behind, and by seeing rivals or situations that act as rivals, you get inspired to do the things that change the world and render it a better place.

The legacy you leave behind will determine how you are remembered. If you leave behind a legacy of kindness, it will inspire others and help them feel appreciated too. Leaving a lasting and significant legacy will allow you to leave something behind that will continue to make a difference after you pass away. If you want to make a difference in the lives of others, consider creating a legacy that will last a lifetime by doing something that has true meaning and that influences thousands of people positively. Leave the world a better place than you found it. Use your rivals to be inspired to change things, so no one else has to face similar people or situations.

While your identity, and the legacy you want to leave behind, help you overcome adversity by giving you a good idea of what you stand for or against, having a vision brings this one step further. More precisely, having a vision makes you realize that life is much longer than you thought and that it has much more to offer than you may think. Having a vision in life is a great way to establish a framework that you can utilize whenever you are facing rivalry. Whether you are facing yourself in the mirror and feel like the reflection is your rival - whereby you are in competition with yourself - or whether it is someone else, a situation, or a challenge you do not know how to overcome, having a vision helps to ground you because you develop a sounding board that you can use to check whether you are living life according to this vision. For example, it makes difficult decisions easier to make: if you aren't sure whether a decision is the right one, you can simply ask yourself, "does this align with my vision?". Usually, the answer is rather decisive.

Your vision refers to the way that you see your life rolling out. It is about how you can foresee your next few years panning out, such as where you think you will be in a few years' time, where you want to be career-wise, how you would like your love life, family life to look, and so on. A vision statement relates to the basic human emotions associated with having a "dream." It grounds you and inspires you to realize your impact on the world. The idea of an idealistic future is a statement of one's own emotional and social future. This is an inspirational vision, and usually, it can be transformed into a statement. However, a well-written vision statement is not the same as a philosophy. It must be realistic and appropriate to your specific view: This is because a vision statement is an inspirational statement that is meant to be used as a sounding board, as mentioned above, and therefore it must be something that you believe is possible. Otherwise, it does not work as you cannot take it seriously and hence don't bother putting work into it.

A vision is important for achieving goals. It presents a relatively clear picture of what you would like the future to look like, which is why it is essential to be flexible on the goals you want to achieve and must be willing to compromise and keep going if certain things do not work out as planned. It should be a compelling vision that is attainable. Whether it is a personal goal or a career goal, a clear vision statement is necessary for a person to achieve their desired outcomes simply because it provides a clear path to follow and an idea of where to go based on your emotions - you have a vision that you want to achieve at all costs, and you are ready to do anything for it. Now you even have a plan for it, but you are ready to change things up slightly in case something comes up and changes the plan you have. Hence, it must be adaptable and flexible to changing circumstances. Ultimately, a well-defined vision statement reflects a person's ideal future as well as varying versions of it. Don't think that the vision won't change. It most likely will. The more you achieve, the more your vision will adapt itself. Life is not linear, and neither is your vision. Adapt it to new goals you are setting for yourself, and don't let yourself get too comfortable. This is how you face your inner rival -you push yourself to get further non-stop!

Once you have a full understanding of the life you live, you start to realize all the important things. You start to see that the rival looking back at you in the mirror is no longer your enemy. Instead, you realize that the reflection of who you created was from all the pain you endured. And now that reflection was only trying to show all the purity you have in you. This new vision gives you something to work towards, something to be proud of, something to look at and think, hell yeah, I did that. It's powerful!

CHAPTER THIRTEEN

SUCCESS MOVES WITH OR WITHOUT THE RIVALRY

Realizing your Potential

In order to succeed at anything, you need to see that you have the potential to reach your goals. For example, if you want to be a recording artist but have no singing ability, having success in this field is not likely. However, if you love working on cars and have a real talent for fixing engines and transmissions, and to you, success would mean working for NASCAR, you have the potential to learn and achieve that success.

Don't Look Back

Everyone has failures or mistakes from the past. To have success, you need to learn from your past and value those difficult lessons but do not ever dwell on the past. Simply move forward and make better, more educated decisions from the lessons learned.

Dare to Dream

To succeed, you need to have dreams and aspirations. Be honest with yourself as to what you want out of life and what you want to give of your life. Allow your mind to dream and think big.

Don't Give Up

To reach success, you have to persevere. Even Thomas Edison had to learn this. When he was creating the incandescent light bulb, it took him more than 10,000 times to get it right. Keep striving even when it becomes challenging.

Have an Unstoppable Attitude

You need to have determination. With good intentions, there may be a close friend or family member that feels it would be better if you focused your attention in another direction. Uphold your unstoppable attitude, determined to succeed.

Stop the Complaining

You might think there is no correlation between complaining and success when in fact, there is a connection. When you are spending time complaining about the obstacles you are facing, you are wasting so much time being negative that you are actually loosing chances to move forward. Instead of thinking of challenges as problems, think of them as opportunities.

Focus on Something you Like

To increase your chance of succeeding, you should concentrate your efforts on something you enjoy. When you start out, make a list of everything you find interesting. Then in a second column, write down the skills you have in relation to each of those items. This will help you narrow choices down based on interest and skill, which gets you started in the right direction for success.

Accept Responsibility

You need to accept responsibility if you make a bad decision or fall behind in your plan. Let us say that you have set some firm milestones that need to be accomplished in order for you to move to the next step. However, you got tired of working hard and took some time to play, which is fine as long as it does not affect your goals. Now months have passed, and you are way behind schedule. This delay has closed several doors of opportunities. Who is to blame?

Be Happy

A positive mind and a happy, upbeat attitude will help you succeed. It has been proven in many studies that a person living in a happy state generally gets much further in just about everything they do. This relates to attitude. Just as a bad attitude can pull you down, a good attitude and a happy, healthy mind will help you meet your objectives.

No Shortcuts

An old cliche states, "Anything worth doing is worth doing well." This should be your motto. When you want to succeed, you cannot afford to take shortcuts. Taking shortcuts leads to imperfection and inadequacies. Always strive for the best, even if it requires a little more time and effort.

Have Courage

Depending on what your specific success is, it may take courage to arrive at your desired destination. For example, if you have a dream of being a writer and to you, that is a success, but according to your long line of family members who have all gone on to be doctors, the only success in their minds is if you follow down the medical path. This means you will have to have the courage to stand up for what you believe and desire to do, even if it means disappointing your family.

Be Excited to Learn

Referring back to the analogy of Edison, when asked about his failures as a young boy, Edison commented, "Young man, I didn't fail 9,999 times; I discovered 9,999 ways not to invent the light bulb." As you work toward your specific success, always enjoy opportunities to learn, even if it takes longer than you think it should.

Share your Success

Although this may be more at the end of the process, it is important. When you finally do reach your success, use your experience to teach, guide, and mentor others so that they too might succeed.

Seek Input

Whatever your idea of success, conduct a "sanity check" throughout the process of reaching your goal. This should be done with someone you trust and who is successful. Ask them to provide honest feedback about your success and as you move through different milestones, bounce concerns or new ideas off them to help keep you on the right track.

Be a Good Listener

To succeed, you need to learn how to listen first. Pay attention to other people who have enjoyed successes in their life, attend seminars given by people that can motivate and encourage, or be open to hearing that a particular idea is not a good one. Good listening takes time to learn, but in the end, it will be your greatest tool.

Be Proactive

While it may take time to learn how to identify ways to avoid obstacles or failures, get into the habit of tackling problems before they arise. This will help you avoid wasting precious time on your road to success.

Stay Motivated

When striving for the big goal of success, it is critical to stay motivated. Find inspiring and motivational tapes, seminars, books, movies, whatever you are able to get your hands on. When you start to feel a little down and out and doubt starts to creep in, turn to these motivational tools to help you keep on track. A few excellent motivators include Tony Robbins, Norman Vincent Peale, Jim Rohn, Zig Ziglar, and Les Brown.

Give Yourself a Break

While being determined is important, do not be so hard on yourself that you become critical of every move you make. Give yourself some room to make mistakes and be flexible with yourself. That does not mean you can miss goals, but it does mean that if you do, you find out how to avoid that from happening again and then get back to work.

Be Passionate

Fall in love with your success. Okay, although that sounds funny, you need to have an intimate passion for your interest. You can do this regardless of what your success is. By having a passion for what you are doing and driving toward, you will automatically put more effort into it. Passion is a good thing as long as it does not become an obsession.

Don't Settle

If you have a goal of becoming a world-famous chef and you know you have both desire and skill, do not just settle to become a short-order cook at your local family style restaurant. While that may be a good training ground, do not allow yourself to lose sight of your ultimate goal.

No Excuses

Many famous actors, music artists, inventors, etc., had special challenges ranging from learning disabilities to physical disabilities. Take Beethoven, for example. He was born deaf, yet he went on to be one of the world's greatest composers or Joni Erickson, who was paralyzed from the neck down, yet she learned to paint with her mouth. Today, her paintings are famous around the world and worth millions. If you are faced with a special challenge of your own, while you may have to adjust things from time to time, do not use excuses. If you want something bad enough, there is a way!

Getting Past Fear of Failure

Being afraid of failure is a normal emotion for every person on the planet. How you get past that fear is the determining factor between failing and succeeding. You can do that by setting realistic goals and then examining those goals on occasion to do any necessary realignment. Above all, believe in yourself and the desire burning within.

Patience and Dues

Succeeding takes time. A goal worth setting will take time to achieve. Be patient with yourself, the people around you, and the process it takes to become successful, also referred to as "paying your dues." Just like the chef scenario, it takes time to be a master chef. Pay your dues by learning and working your way up the ladder to success.

Good Time / Resource Management

Being successful also means keeping to a schedule. In addition, you need to learn how much is too much. Good time and resource management will help you ensure that you use your time wisely and that you are not adding third portions onto a plate still overflowing with seconds.

Attitude

Putting yourself in the right attitude for success should be at the top of your list. Staying positive and surrounding yourself with friends that share a positive attitude will help you succeed. Do not allow negative thoughts to slip into your mind. Attend motivational seminars and find ways to enjoy life. A good attitude will allow you to turn any bad situation into a learning experience. You have heard the saying, "The glass is either half-full or half-empty." You need to adopt the attitude that life is half full. The result is that you will feel better, have more energy, and have a much higher opportunity for success.

Be Thankful

You need to be thankful for not only your accomplishments but also your failures. Having a grateful attitude is important. It will help you stay humble, which in turn will help you continue striving for the ultimate success.

Keep a Journal

As you work hard to reach success, regardless of what you consider that success to be, you need to be able to see your accomplishments. Start a journal and track everything you have conquered. When you feel discouraged or frustrated, reflect on what you have achieved, and rejuvenate yourself.

Rewards

When children do something great, parents will reward them with something nice, whether a kind word of encouragement or a new toy. When people do well in their job, they get raises. As you surpass your milestones, reward yourself. Treat yourself to something nice - a new dress, a new fishing pole, whatever you like. Be sure to award yourself for a job well done.

Make the Best of Each Day

Try to live every day as though it were your last. Make the most of every day and accomplish something. Even if it is something small, every baby step adds up to a huge success in the end.

Make the Process and Adventure

You should look at every angle of your journey as an exciting adventure. When you think of your childhood years, you loved investigating the unknown. Carry this with you as you strive toward success. Anticipate the excitement of each accomplishment - make it a real adventure.

Don't Neglect Things

Especially when things are small and do not appear to have a major impact on the big picture, you need to ensure you follow through and complete your tasks. Those little things can quickly add up to a big mess if not taken care of in a timely and efficient manner.

Offer Praise

If you have people are helping you out, whether on a volunteer basis or a full-time employee, always offer praise. These people are an important part of your success, and by providing praise and support; in return, they will show dedication and work hard to help you reach your goal.

Accept Responsibility

You and you alone are responsible for your success. While you will have help in many instances, the bottom line is that you are responsible. You need to be surrounded by the right people, work with the right investors, going about meeting your success in the right way. It is you that will make the choices and, therefore, your responsibility to make the right choices. In other words, your desire for success must always be greater than any obstacle that stands in your way.

Be Open to Improvement

Sometimes, people get into the habit of thinking they have the answers needed. You need to accept that you do not have all the answers and, more importantly, be open to recommendations from other people. That does not mean you have to agree or even follow those suggestions, but it does mean to listen. You never know when someone will have an idea that will make things easier and more functional, ultimately helping you arrive at your goal more efficiently.

Participate

If attending seminars or lectures that will help you get ahead, if there is the opportunity, participate by asking questions or making valid points. Participation is a great way to remember what is being taught.

Be Serious

Take your efforts to succeed seriously. Success is a serious thing, and it takes serious dedication. You have to have the mindset that this is not going to be all play, at least not in the beginning.

Don't Make Quick Decisions

When things in your plan need to change, unless necessary, do not make quick decisions. Just as it took time to plan in the beginning, it will take time to change. You want to make sure you are making the right decisions when changes come up. Do your research just as you did in the beginning, and then make educated choices.

Avoid Stress

When you strive to be successful, stress is a natural part of the process. Do everything you can to avoid stress. Adding unnecessary stress into the equation will take focus away from accomplishing your goals. You can listen to relaxing tapes, get a professional massage, take a walk, or do whatever helps you to relax. When you start feeling overwhelmed, stop, change direction, and avoid stress. The only thing stress accomplishes is draining your thinking power and creativity.

Be Logical

Okay, you may be thinking that logic itself is logical. However, being logical in many cases means having some level of analytical ability. Regardless of the way you think, find the logic in it. This will help you think and plan clearly and honestly.

Give 100% Effort

If you are going to succeed, you have to be able to get through tough times. You will have to rise to challenges and not quit. You have to plan to go the extra mile and make personal sacrifices. Succeeding means giving 100% effort. Stay focused while keeping your performance on a consistent basis.

Understand your Goal

A great challenge is to prove to yourself that you can do it. One of the ways to prove this to you is to take on responsibility. If your goal for success involves opening a restaurant, work in a restaurant as a server to get a perspective of all the jobs involved to make the restaurant a success. Understand the entire business from the ground up.

Appreciate Life

Do not burn any bridges in life. Appreciate life, people, everything around you. Learn as much as you can from every person you meet. Do not turn people away just because you do not agree with them. You never know; the very people you turn away may be the very people that come to your rescue during a time of difficulty.

CHAPTER FOURTEEN

LETTING GO OF GRUDGES AND BITTERNESS

When someone you care about hurts you, you can hold on to anger, resentment, and thoughts of revenge — or embrace forgiveness and move forward.

Who hasn't been hurt by the actions or words of another? Perhaps a parent constantly criticized you growing up, a colleague sabotaged a project, or your partner had an affair. Or maybe you've had a traumatic experience, such as being physically or emotionally abused by someone close to you.

These wounds can leave you with lasting feelings of anger and bitterness — even vengeance.

But if you don't practice forgiveness, you might be the one who pays most dearly. By embracing forgiveness, you can also embrace peace, hope, gratitude, and joy. Consider how forgiveness can lead you down the path of physical, emotional, and spiritual well-being.

What is forgiveness?

Forgiveness means different things to different people. Generally, however, it involves a decision to let go of resentment and thoughts of revenge.

The act that hurt or offended you might always be with you, but forgiveness can lessen its grip on you and help free you from the control of the person who harmed you. Forgiveness can even lead to feelings of understanding, empathy, and compassion for the one who hurt you.

Forgiveness doesn't mean forgetting or excusing the harm done to you or making up with the person who caused the harm. Forgiveness brings a kind of peace that helps you go on with life.

What are the benefits of forgiving someone?

Letting go of grudges and bitterness can make way for improved health and peace of mind. Forgiveness can lead to:

- Healthier relationships
- Improved mental health
- Less anxiety, stress, and hostility
- Lower blood pressure
- Fewer symptoms of depression
- A stronger immune system
- Improved heart health
- Improved self-esteem

Why is it so easy to hold a grudge?

Being hurt by someone, particularly someone you love and trust, can cause anger, sadness, and confusion. If you dwell on hurtful events or situations, grudges filled with resentment, vengeance and hostility can take root. If you allow negative feelings to crowd out positive feelings, you might find yourself swallowed up by your own bitterness or sense of injustice.

Some people are naturally more forgiving than others. But even if you're a grudge holder, almost anyone can learn to be more forgiving.

What are the effects of holding a grudge?

If you're unforgiving, you might:

- Bring anger and bitterness into every relationship and new experience.
- Become so wrapped up in the wrong that you can't enjoy the present.
- Become depressed or anxious.
- Feel that your life lacks meaning or purpose or that you're at odds with your spiritual beliefs.
- Lose valuable and enriching connectedness with others.

How do I reach a state of forgiveness?

Forgiveness is a commitment to a personalized process of change. To move from suffering to forgiveness, you might:

- Recognize the value of forgiveness and how it can improve your life.
- Identify what needs healing and who needs to be forgiven, and for what.
- Consider joining a support group or seeing a counselor.
- Acknowledge your emotions about the harm done to you and how they affect your behavior, and work to release them
- Choose to forgive the person who's offended you.
- Move away from your role as a victim and release the control and power the offending person and situation have had in your life.

As you let go of grudges, you'll no longer define your life by how you've been hurt. You might even find compassion and understanding.

What happens if I can't forgive someone?

Forgiveness can be challenging, especially if the person who's hurt you doesn't admit wrong. If you find yourself stuck:

- Practice empathy. Try seeing the situation from the other person's point of view.

- Ask yourself why he or she would behave in such away. Perhaps you would have reacted similarly if you faced the same situation.

- Reflect on times you've hurt others and on those who've forgiven you.

- Write in a journal, pray or use guided meditation — or talk with a person you've found to be wise and compassionate, such as a spiritual leader, a mental health provider, or an impartial loved one or friend.

- Be aware that forgiveness is a process, and even small hurts may need to be revisited and forgiven over and over again.

Does forgiveness guarantee reconciliation?

If the hurtful event involved someone whose relationship you otherwise value, forgiveness could lead to reconciliation. This isn't always the case, however.

Reconciliation might be impossible if the offender has died or is unwilling to communicate with you. In other cases, reconciliation might not be appropriate. Still, forgiveness is possible — even if reconciliation isn't.

What if the person I'm forgiving doesn't change?

Getting another person to change his or her actions, behavior, or words isn't the point of forgiveness. Think of forgiveness more about how it can change your life — by bringing you peace, happiness, and emotional and spiritual healing. Forgiveness can take away the power the other person continues to wield in your life.

What if I'm the one who needs forgiveness?

The first step is to honestly assess and acknowledge the wrongs you've done and how they have affected others. Avoid judging yourself too harshly.

If you're truly sorry for something you've said or done, consider admitting it to those you've harmed. Speak of your sincere sorrow or regret, and ask for forgiveness — without making excuses.

Remember, however; you can't force someone to forgive you. Others need to move to forgiveness in their own time. Whatever happens, commit to treating others with compassion, empathy, and respect.

CHAPTER FIFTEEN

SELF-AWARENESS: LEARNING ABOUT YOURSELF TO IMPROVE

The purpose of reflection is to improve practice and become informed in our decisions. Generally, we want to become more able and effective in what we are doing. A lot of reflection is done to make more sense of particular experiences – critical experiences, disorienting dilemmas – however, reflection can also start with the want to develop a better understanding of ourselves.

This doesn't necessarily have to start with an experience but rather a reflective question. To answer this type of question, we will often use experiences as evidence or support.

By learning about ourselves, our motives, and our assumptions, we can develop a toolkit of knowledge and abilities that we can draw on to help ourselves perform to the best of our ability.

Some traits remain stable; others change frequently

Aspects of ourselves like strengths, weaknesses, and values often tend to be fairly consistent over time. That said, they do change naturally, and, of course, with awareness, we can start consciously targeting these elements, for example, by building reflective habits and goals. However, sometimes we might also want to be aware of things that vary faster such as our mood or how we feel about something particular.

The questions and activities you can access from this page will help with awareness of both more stable traits such as strengths and weaknesses and traits that vary more rapidly. They include simple check-in questions we can ask ourselves at the moment and get us to think slightly differently about a problem.

Challenge your answers to remain reflective

One very important aspect of these types of activities and questions is that they lend themselves well to reflection but don't necessarily require a reflective approach. Therefore, to remain reflective, it is important that you challenge your initial instincts and look for evidence – ask yourself 'How do I know?' and 'Why?' regularly.

Example activities and approaches for self-awareness

There are many ways to build self-awareness. The activities and questions available below are not exhaustive but give you a place to start when trying to increase your self-awareness.

1. **Strengths and weaknesses**

   Increasing your self-awareness of your strengths and weaknesses.

   Identifying your strengths and weaknesses can be extremely valuable. Not only will it allow you to approach tasks and challenges with a better understanding of how to succeed and what pitfalls to look out for, but it also allows you to effectively communicate what you can contribute, which is essential for things like job interviews.

How to identify strengths and weaknesses

For all approaches, it can be helpful to set aside a period of undisturbed time where you are fully focused on the task and really probe, for example, 20-30 minutes. Three different approaches are described below – see what you find helpful, add your own, or mix and match them together!

Asking yourself targeted questions

Direct questioning process:

- What is one of my strengths/weaknesses?
- How do I know?
- What does it look like in practice? (For example, if strength is being organized/conscientious, maybe you make lists, keep your desk clean, are always on time, or never miss a deadline.)
- What other strengths/weaknesses may contribute to those behaviors? (For example, the behavior never missing a deadline could come both from being organized and being dedicated.)

Indirect questioning process:

Here are just a few questions to give you an idea – you can likely find many more that are helpful.

- What have others complimented me about? What does that suggest are some of my strengths?
- What have others had to help me with on multiple occasions? Does that tell me anything about any weaknesses I may have?
- What projects/tasks give me or drain my energy? Does the type of activity help inform me about my strengths or weaknesses?

Repeat this process for as many strengths and weaknesses as you can think of. It might be helpful to find a list online of common strengths and weaknesses to give you inspiration.

Analyzing experiences

This approach works for finding both strengths and weaknesses; the only difference is the type of experience you look at. First, identify an experience that turned out/went really well (for strengths) or poorly (for weaknesses). This could be supporting a friend or a teamwork experience that didn't go as you hoped.

- Ask yourself what skills/strengths made you capable of succeeding or what weaknesses may have contributed to an unsuccessful experience.

- Ask yourself what else you could have contributed until you cannot find anymore.

- Repeat for as many experiences as you like.

In reality, this method can be used to identify many implicit aspects of ourselves – the only difference is asking ourselves, 'What [value/assumption/etc.] may have contributed to the outcome of the situation or our actions?'

Asking others

Once you have an idea of your own strengths and weaknesses, or to get you started if you find it challenging, you can ask a critical friend to suggest what they think your strengths and weaknesses are. Remember to reflect on what they say to see if you agree – it is just their opinion and experience, it doesn't necessarily mean they are right. If you don't agree, it is useful to think about why they might experience you in that way.

2. Values

Increasing your self-awareness of your values.

Your values are the things that are important to you. They often take on short labels such as family, friendships, education, personal or professional development.

There are many reasons why knowing your values can be important. Firstly, by explicitly having stated your values, you can assess whether you are spending time and making decisions in accordance with what you find important.

The decisions your values inform will vary in size and complexity. For example, what to do with free time, whether you should prioritize your family over your friends or vice versa, or even whether to work for a company as their values may or may not align with yours. Therefore it can also be very helpful to rank your most important values so that you have a general idea of what to do if you are faced with the dilemma of choosing between two things that are important to you. The context will always be important, but your values can provide you guidance and a starting point.

One important thing to remember is that values will change naturally over time, and therefore even if we decided on aspects of our lives according to our values five years ago, it might not be the right thing for us now. Therefore it is important to actively reflect and challenge our values and habits.

It can be useful to track how you spend your time and see if it matches your values; for example, if friends are important to you, do you show that in your actions?

How to identify personal values

There are many different approaches you can use to identify your personal values. Whichever you choose, it can be helpful to set aside a period of undisturbed time when you are fully focused on the task. Two example approaches are provided below.

Ask yourself questions

One of the easiest ways to identify values is to ask yourself questions like:

- What is important to me?
- What would a perfect day look like? What values are represented in this choice?
- What do I spend my free time on?
- What do I enjoy doing?
- What would I do if there were no limitations?

It can then be helpful to review your answers, consider what values these may represent, and capture all the values on a list.

Once you have a list, it can be beneficial to rank your top 5 or top 10 and save it for reference. If you don't find it easy to rank your values, you can start by trying to identify those at the top of your list by asking yourself questions like 'If I could only have one of these two things in my life, which would I choose?'

Use a word list and narrow it down

This particular approach is adapted from TapRooT's core value identification activity, with the goal of finding your five core values.

Step 1: From the following list, choose and write down values that resonate and are important to you. There is no need to overthink it, but try to be selective, so you don't end up with all of the values on the list. You will likely find that most of the values have some importance to you, so make sure you ask yourself, 'Why this one?' to choose only essential values. If you have a value that is important to you but does not appear on the list, write that one down too.

- Abundance
- Acceptance
- Accountability
- Achievement
- Adventure
- Advocacy
- Ambition
- Appreciation
- Attractiveness
- Autonomy
- Balance

- Being the best
- Benevolence
- Boldness
- Brilliance
- Calmness
- Caring
- Challenge
- Charity
- Cheerfulness
- Cleverness
- Community
- Communication
- Commitment
- Compassion
- Cooperation
- Collaboration
- Consistency
- Contribution
- Creativity
- Credibility
- Curiosity
- Daring
- Decisiveness
- Dedication
- Dependability
- Diversity
- Empathy
- Encouragement
- Engagement
- Enthusiasm
- Ethics
- Excellence

- Expressiveness
- Fairness
- Family
- Friendships
- Flexibility
- Freedom
- Fun
- Generosity
- Grace
- Growth
- Flexibility
- Happiness
- Health
- Honesty
- Humility
- Humour
- Inclusiveness
- Independence
- Individuality
- Innovation
- Inspiration
- Intelligence
- Intuition
- Joy
- Kindness
- Knowledge
- Leadership
- Learning
- Life-long learning
- Love
- Loyalty
- Making a difference

- Mindfulness
- Motivation
- Optimism
- Open-mindedness
- Originality
- Passion
- Performance
- Personal development
- Proactive
- Professionalism
- Quality
- Recognition
- Risk-taking
- Safety
- Security
- Service
- Spirituality
- Stability
- Peace
- Perfection
- Playfulness
- Popularity
- Power
- Preparedness
- Proactivity
- Professionalism
- Punctuality
- Relationships
- Reliability
- Resilience
- Resourcefulness
- Responsibility

- Responsiveness
- Security
- Self-control
- Selflessness
- Simplicity
- Stability
- Success
- Teamwork
- Thankfulness
- Thoughtfulness
- Traditionalism
- Trustworthiness
- Understanding
- Uniqueness
- Usefulness
- Versatility
- Vision
- Warmth
- Wealth
- Wellbeing
- Wisdom
- Zeal

Step 2: Group the values into at most five categories/groupings in a way that makes sense to you. For example, if you selected the values of flexibility and open-mindedness, these might be grouped together as they both have something to do with change. However, it is only important that the groupings make sense for you.

Step 3: Now that you have five groupings, choose one value from each group that functions as an overall label for the group (or make up a label if one value does not stand out). For instance, if you have grouped 'balance,' 'health,' 'personal development,' 'wellbeing,' and 'spirituality,' – the label may end up being 'wellbeing.'

Now you have five core values (or value groups) with a series of important values embedded within these.

Step 4: You can stop the exercise there, or you can choose to add a verb to each of the core values to make it actionable. For instance, to make 'wellbeing' from the above example an actionable value statement, you might make it the actionable value 'Promote wellbeing.'

Step 5: Now challenge yourself to order the core values from most important to least important. Write the prioritized list.

Now you have a list that you can return to for reference when making future decisions.

One challenge with this approach is that it might not support you to make decisions within a value grouping. For example, if you had to choose between supporting a friend or a family member, and both friendships and family are in the same grouping, this method might not help you.

Therefore it can be helpful to make a prioritized list directly from the set of values without grouping them. The questions in the example 'Ask yourself questions' above may be useful to judge the relative importance of the values.

3. Goal setting

Using a reflective approach to set effective goals.

Working toward something tangible can be important for your personal and professional development. While goals are not reflective in their own right, the process of choosing them, developing plans, and identifying challenges and how to overcome them certainly can be very reflective.

There are many different goal-setting models, and it is very important that you find one that works for you. However, there are some common themes across goal-setting models that you should consider:

- **Importance –** ensuring your goal is actually important to you.
- **Specificity –** making your goal specific.
- **Realistic –** making your goal realistic.
- **Planning –** building a robust plan to achieve your goal.
- **Obstacles –** identifying and planning for these.
- **Deadline/Timing –** making it realistic and appropriate.

Each of these is summarized below, along with prompts to ensure you are reflective in the process.

Importance

Many models highlight the importance of finding a goal that is important for you. There might be many things that are important to you, so how do you realize that your goal is essential to you?

You might ask yourself reflective questions such as:

- Why this goal and not something else?
- Is the goal rooted in my values?
- What would it mean for me to complete this goal? Is the result of this goal important?
- How much time am I willing to give to obtain this goal? Does is it feel an appropriate amount of time for how important I think the goal is?

Specificity

Goals need to be sufficiently specific so that you know when you have achieved them.

For instance, a common goal might be to 'get better at X,' but how do you know you have gotten better? Is it when someone else recognizes it? Is it a feeling? Is it learning one fact about the thing you want to improve on?

To ensure specificity, the main questions you need to ask yourself are something like:

- What is my finish line?

- How will I know I have accomplished my goal?

- How will it feel? Will I be able to recognize the feeling?

- How does it usually look and feel when I accomplish something? How could you define your goal so that you will feel this way about achieving it?

- Am I specific about all aspects or only a few of them? For instance, I might be specific about what it will look like, but am I specific about when it should be done?

Checking that your goal is realistic

It can be important to have big dreams, but being realistic is essential for being successful – so have you been realistic? You can ask yourself questions like:

- Is it possible to accomplish my goal in the time I have available?

- Based on my previous experiences, does it seem likely I will be successful?

- Do I have a tendency to be optimistic about how easy some things are? Do I underestimate the time it will take to complete tasks or projects? If that's the case, does know that inform me about how realistic the goal is?

Ensuring that you have a robust plan

As important as it is to know where you want to finish, it is equally important to know how to get there with a robust plan. To ensure you have tested your plan, ask yourself questons like:

- When planning, have I looked at my situation from enough perspectives?

- Do I have past experiences that can help inform my current planning?

- How will I deal with unforeseen challenges?

- Have I made the best attempt I can to foresee potential challenges and find ways to offset them? If not, what challenges do I need to plan for?

- If I had to find one weakness in my plan, what would it be? How can I fix that?

Identifying and figuring out how to deal with obstacles

On the way to accomplishing your goal, you will likely experience obstacles – both internal and external. To increase your chance of success, it is important to identify known or potential obstacles and plan how to deal with them. Ask yourself questions like:

- Which of my weaknesses will become a challenge to my fulfilling this goal?

- If everything goes wrong, what will be the thing that will make it least likely for me to get back on track? How can I mitigate that risk?

- What do my experiences tell me about how I myself may make achieving this goal difficult or challenging? For instance, it might be a tendency to postpone tasks or to lose focus.

- Which of my strengths will be useful in overcoming these challenges?

- Do I need to rework my plan to account for some of these challenges?

- What support do I have?

Make sure that the deadline for your goal is realistic and appropriate

When you reflect on the aspects that make up the goal and your plans for getting there, ensure that you give yourself enough time to achieve the goal. Equally, avoid giving yourself too much time as this can lead to procrastination and lack of focus. Ask yourself:

- Based on my plan, my obstacles, and my experiences, what is a realistic timescale for me to achieve my goal?

- If you already have set a deadline, ask yourself if you would be able to accomplish your goal in less time. Would you be able to do it if you had one day less? One week less? One month less?

By being reflective when setting your goals, you will help yourself to optimize your chance of being successful.

CONCLUSION

On that note, this concludes the book. Ultimately, what you believe is your biggest rival or abo, if it is a person, is where you want to start. Your rivals, whether they are people, situations, or events, will either break you or will push you upwards. You are born with a form of rivalry as you compete with yourself. You holding this very book is proof of this. Your rival may also be time or making the right decisions. It may be someone cancerous, such as a toxic friend or relationship. It may be finding who you are or your own identity: You may, indeed, be your own rival. Thus, find out who you are rivaling against, and you can get started on your journey towards leaving behind a legacy that fits your life vision.

Sincerely,

Author.

www.ingramcontent.com/pod-product-compliance
Lightning Source LLC
LaVergne TN
LVHW052047160826
845678LV00015B/3129